The Power of Truth

William George Jordan

Table of Contents

1. The Power of Truth

Truth is the rock foundation of every great character. It is loyalty to the right as we see it; it is courageous living of our lives in harmony with our ideals; it is always—power.

Truth ever defies full definition. Like electricity it can only be explained by noting its manifestation. It is the compass of the soul, the guardian of conscience, the final touchstone of right. Truth is the revelation of the ideal; but it is also an inspiration to realize that ideal, a constant impulse to live it.

Lying is one of the oldest vices in the world—it made its début in the first recorded conversation in history, in a famous interview in the garden of Eden. Lying is the sacrifice of honor to create a wrong impression. It is masquerading in misfit virtues. Truth can stand alone, for it needs no chaperone or escort. Lies are cowardly, fearsome things that must travel in battalions. They are like a lot of drunken men, one vainly seeking to support another. Lying is the partner and accomplice of all the other vices. It is the cancer of moral degeneracy in an individual life.

Truth is the oldest of all the virtues; it antedated man, it lived before there was man to perceive it or to accept it. It is the unchangeable, the constant.

Law is the eternal truth of Nature—the unity that always produces identical results under identical conditions. When a man discovers a great truth in Nature he has the key to the understanding of a million phenomena; when he grasps a great truth in morals he has in it the key to his spiritual re-creation. For the individual, there is no such thing as theoretic truth; a great truth that is not absorbed by our whole mind and life, and has not become an inseparable part of our living, is not a real truth to us. If we know the truth and do not live it, our life is —a lie.

In speech, the man who makes Truth his watchword is careful in his words, he seeks to be accurate, neither understating nor over-coloring. He never states as a fact that of which he is not sure. What he says has the ring of sincerity, the hallmark of pure gold. If he praises you, you accept his statement as "net," you do not have to work out a problem in mental arithmetic on the side to see what discount you ought to make before you accept his judgment. His promise counts for something, you accept it as being as good as his bond, you know that no matter how much it may cost him to verify and fulfil his word by his deed, he will do it. His honesty is not policy. The man who is honest merely because it is "the best policy," is not really honest, he is only politic. Usually such a man would forsake his seeming loyalty to truth and would work overtime for the devil—if he could get better terms.

Truth means "that which one troweth or believes." It is living simply and squarely by our belief; it is the externalizing of a faith in a series of actions. Truth is ever strong, courageous, virile, though kindly, gentle, calm, and restful. There is a vital difference between error and untruthfulness. A man may be in error and yet live bravely by it; he who is untruthful in his life knows the truth but denies it. The one is loyal to what he believes, the other is traitor to what he knows.

"What is Truth?" Pilate's great question, asked of Christ nearly two thousand years ago, has echoed unanswered through the ages. We get constant revelations of parts of it, glimpses of constantly new phases, but never complete, final definition. If we but live up to the truth that we know, and seek ever to know more, we have put ourselves into the spiritual attitude of receptiveness to know Truth in the fullness of its power. Truth is the sun of morality, and like that lesser sun in the heavens, we can walk by its light, live in its warmth and life, even if we see but a small part of it and receive but a microscopic fraction of its rays.

Which of the great religions of the world is the real, the final, the absolute truth? We must make our individual choice and live by it as best we can. Every new sect, every new cult, has in it a grain of truth, at least; it is this that attracts attention and wins adherents. This mustard seed of truth is often overestimated, darkening the eyes of man to the untrue parts or phases of the varying religious faiths. But, in exact proportion to the basic truth they contain do religions last, become permanent and growing, and satisfy and inspire the hearts of men. Mushrooms of error have a quick growth, but they exhaust their vitality and die, while Truth still lives.

The man who makes the acquisition of wealth the goal and ultimatum of his life, seeing it as an end rather than a means to an end, is not true. Why does the world usually make wealth the criterion of success, and riches the synonym of attainment? Real success in life means the individual's conquest of himself; it means "how he has bettered himself" not "how he has bettered his fortune." The great question of life is not "What have I?" but "What am I?"

Man is usually loyal to what he most desires. The man who lies to save a nickel, merely proclaims that he esteems a nickel more than he does his honor. He who sacrifices his ideals, truth and character, for mere money or position, is weighing his conscience in one pan of a scale against a bag of gold in the other. He is loyal to what he finds the heavier, that which he desires the more—the money. But this is not truth. Truth is the heart's loyalty to abstract right, made manifest in concrete instances.

The tradesman who lies, cheats, misleads and overcharges and then seeks to square himself with his anæmic conscience by saying, "lying is absolutely necessary to business," is as untrue in his statement as he is in his acts. He justifies himself with the petty defence as the thief who says it is necessary to steal in order to live. The permanent business prosperity of an individual, a city or a nation rests finally on commercial integrity alone, despite all that the cynics may say, or all the exceptions whose temporary success may mislead them. It is truth alone that lasts.

The politician who is vacillating, temporizing, shifting, constantly trimming his sails to catch every puff of wind of popularity, is a trickster who succeeds only until he is found out. A lie may live for a time, truth for all time. A lie never lives by its own vitality, it merely continues to exist because it simulates truth. When it is unmasked, it dies.

When each of four newspapers in one city puts forth the claim that its circulation is larger than all the others combined, there must be an error somewhere. Where there is untruth there is always conflict, discrepancy, impossibility. If all the truths of life and experience from the first second of time, or for any section of eternity, were brought together, there would be perfect harmony, perfect accord, union and unity, but if two lies come together, they quarrel and seek to destroy each other.

It is in the trifles of daily life that truth should be our constant guide and inspiration. Truth is not a dress-suit, consecrated to special occasions, it is the strong, well-woven, durable homespun for daily living.

The man who forgets his promises is untrue. We rarely lose sight of those promises made to us for our individual benefit; these we regard as checks we always seek to cash at the earliest moment. "The miser never forgets where he hides his treasure," says one of the old philosophers. Let us cultivate that sterling honor that holds our word so supreme, so sacred, that to forget it would seem a crime, to deny it would be impossible.

The man who says pleasant things and makes promises which to him are light as air, but to someone else seem the rock upon which a life's hope is built is cruelly untrue. He who does not regard his appointments, carelessly breaking them or ignoring them, is the thoughtless thief of another's time. It reveals selfishness, carelessness, and lax business morals. It is untrue to the simplest justice of life.

Men who split hairs with their conscience, who mislead others by deft, shrewd phrasing which may be true in letter yet lying in spirit and designedly uttered to produce a false impression, are untruthful in the most cowardly way. Such men would cheat even in solitaire. Like murderers they forgive themselves their crime in congratulating themselves on the cleverness of their alibi.

The parent who preaches honor to his child and gives false statistics about the child's age to the conductor, to save a nickel, is not true.

The man who keeps his religion in camphor all week and who takes it out only on Sunday, is not true. He who seeks to get the highest wages for the least possible amount of service, is not true. The man who has to sing lullabies to his conscience before he himself can sleep, is not true.

Truth is the straight line in morals. It is the shortest distance between a fact and the expression of it. The foundations of truth should ever be laid in childhood. It is then that parents should instil into the young mind the instant, automatic turning to truth, making it the constant atmosphere of the mind and life. Let the child know that "Truth above all things" should be the motto of its life. Parents make a great mistake when they look upon a lie as a disease in morals; it is not always a disease in itself, it is but a symptom. Behind every untruth is some reason, some cause, and it is this cause that should be removed. The lie may be the result of fear, the attempt to cover a fault and to escape punishment; it may be merely the evidence of an over-active imagination; it may reveal maliciousness or obstinacy; it may be the hunger for praise that leads the child to win attention and to startle others by wonderful stories; it may be merely carelessness in speech, the reckless use of words; it may be acquisitiveness that makes lying the handmaid of theft. But if, in the life of the child or the adult, the symptom be made to reveal the disease, and that be then treated, truth reasserts itself and the moral health is restored.

Constantly telling a child not to lie is giving life and intensity to "the lie." The true method is to quicken the moral muscles from the positive side, urge the child to be honest, to be faithful, to be loyal, to be fearless to the truth. Tell him ever of the nobility of courage to speak the true, to live the right, to hold fast to principles of honor in every trifle—then he need never fear to face any of life's crises.

The parent must live truth or the child will not live it. The child will startle you with its quickness in puncturing the bubble of your pretended knowledge; in instinctively piercing the heart of a sophistry without being conscious of process; in relentlessly enumerating your unfulfilled promises; in detecting with the justice of a court of equity a technicality of speech that is virtually a lie. He will justify his own lapses from truth by appeal to some white lie told to a visitor, and unknown to be overheard by the little one, whose mental powers we ever underestimate in theory though we may overpraise in words.

Teach the child in a thousand ways, directly and indirectly, the power of truth, the beauty of truth, and the sweetness and rest of companionship with truth.

And if it be the rock-foundation of the child character, as a fact, not as a theory, the future of that child is as fully assured as it is possible for human prevision to guarantee.

The power of Truth, in its highest, purest, and most exalted phases, stands squarely on four basic lines of relation,—the love of truth, the search for truth, faith in truth, and work for truth.

The love of Truth is the cultivated hunger for it in itself and for itself, without any thought of what it may cost, what sacrifices it may entail, what theories or beliefs of a lifetime may be laid desolate. In its supreme phase, this attitude of life is rare, but unless one can begin to put himself into harmony with this view, the individual will only creep in truth, when he might walk bravely. With the love of truth, the individual scorns to do a mean thing, no matter what be the gain, even if the whole world would approve. He would not sacrifice the sanction of his own high standard for any gain, he would not willingly deflect the needle of his thought and act from the true North, as he knows it, by the slightest possible variation. He himself would know of the deflection—that would be enough. What matters it what the world thinks if he have his own disapproval?

The man who has a certain religious belief and fears to discuss it, lest it may be proved wrong, is not loyal to his belief, he has but a coward's faithfulness to his prejudices. If he were a lover of truth, he would be willing at any moment to surrender his belief for a higher, better, and truer faith.

The man who votes the same ticket in politics, year after year, without caring for issues, men, or problems, merely voting in a certain way because he always has voted so, is sacrificing loyalty to truth to a weak, mistaken, stubborn attachment to a worn-out precedent. Such a man should stay in his cradle all his life—because he spent his early years there.

The search for Truth means that the individual must not merely follow truth as he sees it, but he must, so far as he can, search to see that he is right. When the Kearsarge was wrecked on the Roncador Reef, the captain was sailing correctly by his chart. But his map was an old one; the sunken reef was not marked down. Loyalty to back-number standards means stagnation. In China they plow to-day, but they plow with the instrument of four thousand years ago. The search for truth is the angel of progress—in civilization and in morals. While it makes us bold and aggressive in our own life, it teaches us to be tender and sympathetic with others. Their life may represent a station we have passed in our progress, or one we must seek to reach. We can then congratulate ourselves without condemning them. All the truths of the world are not concentrated in our creed. All the sunshine of the world is not focused on our doorstep. We should ever speak the truth,—but only in love and kindness. Truth should ever extend the hand of love; never the hand clenching a bludgeon.

Faith in Truth is an essential to perfect companionship with truth. The individual must have perfect confidence and assurance of the final triumph of right, and order, and justice, and believe that all things are evolving toward that divine consummation, no matter how dark and dreary life may seem from day to day. No real success, no lasting happiness can exist except it be founded on the rock of truth. The prosperity that is based on lying, deception, and intrigue, is only temporary—it cannot last any more than a mushroom can outlive an oak. Like the blind Samson, struggling in the temple, the individual whose life is based on trickery always pulls down the supporting columns of his own edifice, and perishes in the ruins. No matter what price a man may pay for truth, he is getting it at a bargain. The lying of others can never hurt us long, it always carries with it our exoneration in the end. During the siege of Sebastopol, the Russian shells that threatened to destroy a fort opened a hidden spring of water in the hillside, and saved the thirsting people they sought to kill.

Work for the interests and advancement of Truth is a necessary part of real companionship. If a man has a love of truth, if he searches to find it, and has faith in it, even when he cannot find it, will he not work to spread it? The strongest way for man to strengthen the power of truth in the world is to live it himself in every detail of thought, word, and deed—to make himself a sun of personal radiation of truth, and to let his silent influence speak for it and his direct acts glorify it so far as he can in his sphere of life and action. Let him first seek to be, before he seeks to teach or to do, in any line of moral growth.

Let man realize that Truth is essentially an intrinsic virtue, in his relation to himself even if there were no other human being living; it becomes extrinsic as he radiates it in his daily life. Truth is first, intellectual honesty—the craving to know the right; second, it is moral honesty, the hunger to live the right.

Truth is not a mere absence of the vices. This is only a moral vacuum. Truth is the living, pulsing breathing of the virtues of life. Mere refraining from wrong-doing is but keeping the weeds out of the garden of one's life. But this must be followed by positive planting of the seeds of right to secure the flowers of true living. To the negatives of the Ten Commandments must be added the positives of the Beatitudes. The one condemns, the other commends; the one forbids, the other inspires; the one emphasizes the act, the other the spirit behind the act. The whole truth rests not in either, but in both.

A man cannot truly believe in God without believing in the final inevitable triumph of Truth. If you have Truth on your side you can pass through the dark valley of slander, misrepresentation and abuse, undaunted, as though you wore a magic suit of mail that no bullet could enter, no arrow could pierce. You can hold your head high, toss it fearlessly and defiantly, look every man calmly and unflinchingly in the eye, as though you rode, a victorious king, returning at the head of your legions with banners waving and lances glistening, and bugles filling the air with music. You can feel the great expansive wave of moral health surging through you as the quickened blood courses through the body of him who is gladly, gloriously proud of physical health. You will know that all will come right in the end, that it must come, that error must flee before the great white light of truth, as darkness slinks away into nothingness in the presence of the sunburst. Then, with Truth as your guide, your companion, your ally, and inspiration, you tingle with the consciousness of your kinship with the Infinite and all the petty trials, sorrows and sufferings of life fade away like temporary, harmless visions seen in a dream.

2. The Courage to Face Ingratitude

Ingratitude, the most popular sin of humanity, is forgetfulness of the heart. It is the revelation of the emptiness of pretended loyalty. The individual who possesses it finds it the shortest cut to all the other vices.

Ingratitude is a crime more despicable than revenge, which is only returning evil for evil, while ingratitude returns evil for good. People who are ungrateful rarely forgive you if you do them a good turn. Their microscopic hearts resent the humiliation of having been helped by a superior, and this rankling feeling filtering through their petty natures often ends in hate and treachery.

Gratitude is thankfulness expressed in action. It is the instinctive radiation of justice, giving new life and energy to the individual from whom it emanates. It is the heart's recognition of kindness that the lips cannot repay. Gratitude never counts its payments. It realizes that no debt of kindness can ever be outlawed, ever be cancelled, ever paid in full. Gratitude ever feels the insignificance of its instalments; ingratitude the nothingness of the debt. Gratitude is the flowering of a seed of kindness;

ingratitude is the dead inactivity of a seed dropped on a stone.

The expectation of gratitude is human; the rising superior to ingratitude is almost divine. To desire recognition of our acts of kindness and to hunger for appreciation and the simple justice of a return of good for good, is natural. But man never rises to the dignity of true living until he has the courage that dares to face ingratitude calmly, and to pursue his course unchanged when his good works meet with thanklessness or disdain.

Man should have only one court of appeals as to his actions, not "what will be the result?" "how will it be received?" but "is it right?" Then he should live his life in harmony with this standard alone, serenely, bravely, loyally and unfalteringly, making "right for right's sake" both his ideal and his inspiration.

Man should not be an automatic gas-machine, cleverly contrived to release a given quantity of illumination under the stimulus of a nickel. He should be like the great sun itself which ever radiates light, warmth, life and power, because it cannot help doing so, because these qualities fill the heart of the sun, and for it to have them means that it must give them constantly. Let the sunlight of our sympathy, tenderness, love, appreciation, influence and kindness ever go out from us as a glow to brighten and hearten others. But do not let us ever spoil it all by going through life constantly collecting receipts, as vouchers, to stick on the file of our self-approval.

It is hard to see those who have sat at our board in the days of our prosperity, flee as from a pestilence when misfortune darkens our doorway; to see the loyalty upon which we would have staked our life, that seemed firm as a rock, crack and splinter like thin glass at the first real test; to know that the fire of friendship at which we could ever warm our hands in our hour of need, has turned to cold, dead, gray ashes, where warmth is but a haunting memory.

To realize that he who once lived in the sanctuary of our affection, in the frank confidence where conversation seemed but our soliloquy, and to whom our aims and aspirations have been thrown open with no Bluebeard chamber of reserve, has been secretly poisoning the waters of our reputation and undermining us by his lies and treachery, is hard indeed. But no matter how the ingratitude stings us, we should just swallow the sob, stifle the tear, smile serenely and bravely, and—seek to forget.

In justice to ourselves we should not permit the ingratitude of a few to make us condemn the whole world. We pay too much tribute to a few human insects when we let their wrong-doing paralyze our faith in humanity. It is a lie of the cynics that says "all men are ungrateful," a companion lie to "all men have their price." We must trust humanity if we would get good from humanity. He who thinks all mankind is vile is a pessimist who mistakes his introspection for observation; he looks into his own heart and thinks he sees the world. He is like a cross-eyed man, who never sees what he seems to be looking at.

Confidence and credit are the cornerstones of business, as they are of society. Withdraw them from business and the activities and enterprises of the world would stop in an instant, topple and fall into chaos. Withdraw confidence in humanity from the individual, and he becomes but a breathing, selfish egotist, the one good man left, working overtime in nursing his petty grudge against the world because a few whom he has favored have been ungrateful.

If a man receives a counterfeit dollar he does not straightway lose his faith in all money,—at least there are no such instances on record in this country. If he has a run of three or four days of dull weather he does not say "the sun ceases to exist, there are surely no bright days to come in the whole calendar of time."

If a man's breakfast is rendered an unpleasant memory by some item of food that has outlived its usefulness, he does not forswear eating. If a man finds under a tree an apple with a suspicious looking hole on one side, he does not condemn the whole orchard; he simply confines his criticism to that apple. But he who has helped some one who, later, did not pass a good examination on gratitude, says in a voice plaintive with the consciousness of injury, and with a nod of his head that implies the wisdom of Solomon: "I have had my experience, I have learned my lesson. This is the last time I will have faith in any man. I did this for him, and that for him, and now, look at the result!"

Then he unrolls a long schedule of favors, carefully itemized and added up, till it seems the pay-roll of a great city. He complains of the injustice of one man, yet he is willing to be unjust to the whole world, making it bear the punishment of the wrong of an individual. There is too much vicarious suffering already in this earth of ours without this lilliputian attempt to extend it by syndicating one man's ingratitude. If one man drinks to excess, it is not absolute justice to send the whole world to jail.

The farmer does not expect every seed that he sows in hope and faith to fall on good ground and bring forth its harvest; he is perfectly certain that this will not be so, cannot be. He is counting on the final outcome of many seeds, on the harvest of all, rather than on the harvest of one. If you really want gratitude, and must have it, be willing to make many men your debtors.

The more unselfish, charitable and exalted the life and mission of the individual, the larger will be the number of instances of ingratitude that must be met and vanquished. The thirty years of Christ's life was a tragedy of ingratitudes. Ingratitude is manifest in three degrees of intensity in the world—He knew them all in numberless bitter instances.

The first phase, the simplest and most common, is that of thoughtless thanklessness, as was shown in the case of the ten lepers healed in one day—nine departed without a word, only one gave thanks.

The second phase of ingratitude is denial, a positive sin, not the mere negation of thanklessness. This was exemplified in Peter, whose selfish desire to stand well with two maids and some bystanders, in the hour when he had the opportunity to be loyal to Christ, forgot his friendship, lost all thought of his indebtedness to his Master, and denied Him, not once or twice, but three times.

The third phase of ingratitude is treachery, where selfishness grows vindictive, as shown by Judas, the honored treasurer of the little band of thirteen, whose jealousy, ingratitude, and thirty pieces of silver, made possible the tragedy of Calvary.

These three—thanklessness, denial and treachery— run the gamut of ingratitude, and the first leads to the second, and the second prepares the way for the third.

We must ever tower high above dependence on human gratitude or we can do nothing really great, nothing truly noble. The expectation of gratitude is the alloy of an otherwise virtuous act. It ever dulls the edge of even our best actions. Most persons look at gratitude as a protective tariff on virtues. The man who is weakened in well-doing by the ingratitude of others, is serving God on a salary basis. He is a hired soldier, not a volunteer. He should be honest enough to see that he is working for a reward; like a child, he is being good for a bonus. He is really regarding his kindness and his other expressions of goodness as moral stock he is willing to hold only so long as they pay dividends.

There is in such living always a touch of the pose; it is waiting for the applause of the gallery. We must let the consciousness of doing right, of living up to our ideals, be our reward and stimulus, or life will become to us but a series of failures, sorrows and disappointments.

Much of the seeming ingratitude in life comes from our magnifying of our own acts, our minifying of the acts of others. We may have overestimated the importance of something that we have done; it may have been most trivial, purely incidental, yet the marvellous working of the loom of time brought out great and unexpected results to the recipient of our favor. We often feel that wondrous gratitude is due us, though we were in no wise the inspiration of the success we survey with such a feeling of pride. A chance introduction given by us on the street may, through an infinity of circumstances, make our friend a millionaire. Thanks may be due us for the introduction, and perhaps not even that, for it might have been unavoidable, but surely we err when we expect him to be meekly grateful to us for his subsequent millions.

The essence of truest kindness lies in the grace with which it is performed. Some men seem to discount all gratitude, almost make it impossible, by the way in which they grant favors. They make you feel so small, so mean, so inferior; your cheeks burn with indignation in the acceptance of the boon you seek at their hands. You feel it is like a bone thrown at a dog, instead of the quick, sympathetic graciousness that forestalls your explanations and waives your thanks with a smile, the pleasure of one friend who has been favored with the opportunity to be of service to another. The man who makes another feel like an insect reclining on a red-hot stove while he is receiving a favor, has no right to expect future gratitude,—he should feel satisfied if he receives forgiveness.

Let us forget the good deeds we have done by making them seem small in comparison with the greater things we are doing, and the still greater acts we hope to do. This is true generosity, and will develop gratitude in the soul of him who has been helped, unless he is so petrified in selfishness as to make it impossible. But constantly reminding a man of the favors he has received from you almost cancels the debt. The care of the statistics should be his privilege; you are usurping his prerogative when you recall them. Merely because it has been our good fortune to be able to serve some one, we should not act as if we held a mortgage on his immortality, and expect him to swing the censor of adulation forever in our presence.

That which often seems to us to be ingratitude, may be merely our own ignorance of the subtle phases of human nature. Sometimes a man's heart is so full of thankfulness that he cannot speak, and in the very intensity of his appreciation, mere words seem to him paltry, petty, and inadequate, and the depth of the eloquence of his silence is misunderstood. Sometimes the consciousness of his inability to repay, develops a strange pride—genuine gratitude it may be, though unwise in its lack of expression—a determination to say nothing, until the opportunity for which he is waiting to enable him to make his gratitude an actuality. There are countless instances in which true gratitude has all the semblance of the basest ingratitude, as certain harmless plants are made by Nature to resemble poison-ivy.

Ingratitude is some one's protest that you are no longer necessary to him; it is often the expression of rebellion at the discontinuance of favors. People are rarely ungrateful until they have exhausted their assessments. Profuse expressions of gratitude do not cancel an indebtedness any more than a promissory note settles an account. It is a beginning, not a finality. Gratitude that is extravagant in words is usually economical in all other expression.

No good act performed in the world ever dies. Science tells us that no atom of matter can ever be destroyed, that no force once started ever ends; it merely passes through a multiplicity of ever-changing phases. Every good deed done to others is a great force that starts an unending pulsation through time and eternity. We may not know it, we may never hear a word of gratitude or of recognition, but it will all come back to us in some form as naturally, as perfectly, as inevitably, as echo answers to sound. Perhaps not as we expect it, how we expect it, nor where, but sometime, somehow, somewhere, it comes back, as the dove that Noah sent from the Ark returned with its green leaf of revelation.

Let us conceive of gratitude in its largest, most beautiful sense, that if we receive any kindness we are debtor, not merely to one man, but to the whole world. As we are each day indebted to thousands for the comforts, joys, consolations, and blessings of life, let us realize that it is only by kindness to all that we can begin to repay the debt to one, begin to make gratitude the atmosphere of all our living and a constant expression in outward acts, rather than in mere thoughts. Let us see the awful cowardice and the injustice of ingratitude, not to take it too seriously in others, not to condemn it too severely, but merely to banish it forever from our own lives, and to make every hour of our living the radiation of the sweetness of gratitude.

3. People who Live in Air Castles

Living in an air-castle is about as profitable as owning a half-interest in a rainbow. It is no more nourishing than a dinner of twelve courses—eaten in a dream. Air-castles are built of golden moments of time, and their only value is in the raw material thus rendered valueless.

The atmosphere of air-castles is heavy and stupefying with the incense of vague hopes and phantom ideals. In them man lulls himself into dreaming inactivity with the songs of the mighty deeds he is going to do, the great influence he some day will have, the vast wealth that will be his, sometime, somehow, somewhere, in the rosy, sunlit days of the future. The architectural error about air-castles is that the owner builds them downward from their gilded turrets in the clouds, instead of upward from a solid, firm foundation of purpose and energy. This diet of mental lotus-leaves is a mental narcotic, not a stimulant.

Ambition, when wedded to tireless energy is a great thing and a good thing, but in itself it amounts to little. Man cannot raise himself to higher things by what he would like to accomplish, but only by what he endeavors to accomplish. To be of value, ambition must ever be made manifest in zeal, in determination, in energy consecrated to an ideal. If it be thus reinforced, thus combined, the thin airy castle melts into nothingness, and the individual stands on a new strong foundation of solid rock, whereon, day by day and stone by stone, he can rear a mighty material structure of life-work to last through time and eternity. The air-castle ever represents the work of an architect without a builder; it means plans never put into execution. They tell us that man is the architect of his own fortunes. But if he be merely architect he will make only an air-castle of his life; he should be architect and builder too.

Living in the future is living in an air-castle. To-morrow is the grave where the dreams of the dreamer, the toiler who toils not, are buried. The man who says he will lead a newer and better life to-morrow, who promises great things for the future, and yet does nothing in the present to make that future possible, is living in an air-castle. In his arrogance he is attempting to perform a miracle; he is seeking to turn water into wine, to have harvest without seed-time, to have an end without a beginning.

If we would make our lives worthy of us, grand and noble, solid and impregnable, we must forsake air-castles of dreaming for strongholds of doing. Every man with an ideal has a right to live in the glow and inspiration of it, and to picture the joy of attainment, as the tired traveller fills his mind with the thought of the brightness of home, to quicken his steps and to make the weary miles seem shorter, but the worker should never really worry about the future, think little of it except for inspiration, to determine his course, as mariners study the stars, to make his plans wisely and to prepare for that future by making each separate day the best and truest that he can.

Let us live up to the fulness of our possibilities each day. Man has only one day of life—to-day. He did live yesterday, he may live to-morrow, but he has only to-day.

The secret of true living—mental, physical and moral, material and spiritual,—may be expressed in five words: Live up to your portion. This is the magic formula that transforms air-castles into fortresses.

Men sometimes grow mellow and generous in the thought of what they would do if great wealth came to them. "If I were a millionaire," they say,—and they let the phrase melt sweetly in their mouths as though it were a caramel,—"I would subsidize genius; I would found a college; I would build a great hospital; I would erect model tenements; I would show the world what real charity is." Oh, it is all so easy, so easy, this vicarious benevolence, this spending of other people's fortunes! Few of us, according to the latest statistics, have a million, but we all have something, some part of it. Are we living up to our portion? Are we generous with what we have?

The man who is selfish with one thousand dollars will not develop angelic wings of generosity when his million comes. If the generous spirit be a reality with the individual, instead of an empty boast, he will, every hour, find opportunity to make it manifest. The radiation of kindness need not be expressed in money at all. It may be shown in a smile of human interest, a glow of sympathy, a word of fellowship with the sorrowing and the struggling, an instinctive outstretching of a helping hand to one in need.

No man living is so poor that he cannot evidence his spirit of benevolence toward his fellowman. It may assume that rare and wondrously beautiful phase of divine charity, in realizing how often a motive is misrepresented in the act, how sin, sorrow and suffering have warped and disguised latent good, in substituting a word of gentle tolerance for some cheap tinsel of shabby cynicism that pretends to be wit. If we are not rich enough to give "cold, hard" cash, let us at least be too rich to give "cold, hard" words. Let us leave our air-castles of vague self-adulation for so wisely spending millions we have never seen, and rise to the dignity of living up to the full proportion of our possessions, no matter how slight they may be. Let us fill the world around us with love, brightness, sweetness, gentleness, helpfulness, courage and sympathy, as if they were the only legal tender and we were Monte Cristos with untold treasures of such gold ever at our call.

Let us cease saying: "If I were," and say ever: "I am." Let us stop living in the subjunctive mood, and begin to live in the indicative.

The one great defence of humanity against the charge of unfulfilled duties is "lack of time." The constant clamoring for time would be pathetic, were it not for the fact that most individuals throw away more of it than they use. Time is the only really valuable possession of man, for without it every power within him would cease to exist. Yet he recklessly squanders his great treasure as if it were valueless. The wealth of the whole world could not buy one second of time. Yet Society assassins dare to say in public that they have been "killing time." The time fallacy has put more people into air-castles than all other causes combined. Life is only time; eternity is only more time; immortality is merely man's right to live through unending time.

"If I had a library I would read," is the weak plaint of some other tenant of an air-castle. If a man does not read the two or three good books in his possession or accessible to him he would not read if he had the British Museum brought to his bedside, and the British Army delegated to continual service in handing him books from the shelves. The time sacrificed to reading sensational newspapers might be consecrated to good reading, if the individual were willing merely to live up to his portion of opportunity.

The man who longs for some crisis in life, wherein he may show mighty courage, while he is expending no portion of that courage in bearing bravely the petty trials, sorrows and disappointments of daily life, is living in an air-castle. He is just a sparrow looking enviously at the mountain crags where the hardy eagle builds her nest, and dreaming of being a great bird like that, perhaps even daring in a patronizing way, to criticise her method of flight and to plume himself with the medals he could win for flying if he only would. It is the day-by-day heroism that vitalizes all of a man's power in an emergency, that gives him confidence that when need comes he will and must be ready.

The air-castle typifies any delusion or folly that makes man forsake real living for an idle, vague existence. Living in air-castles means that a man sees life in a wrong perspective. He permits his lower self to dominate his higher self; he who should tower as a mighty conqueror over the human weakness, sin and folly that threaten to destroy his better nature, binds upon his own wrists the manacles of habit that hold him a slave. He loses the crown of his kingship because he sells his royal birthright for temporary ease and comfort and the showy things of the world, sacrificing so much that is best in him for mere wealth, success, position, or the plaudits of the world. He forsakes the throne of individuality for the air-castle of delusion.

The man who wraps himself in the Napoleonic cloak of his egotism, hypnotizing himself into believing that he is superior to all other men, that the opera-glasses of the universe are focused upon him and that he treads the stage alone, had better wake up. He is living in an air-castle. He who, like Narcissus, falls in love with his own reflection and thinks he has a monopoly of the great work of the world, whose conceit rises from him like the smoke from the magic bottle of the genii and spreads till it shuts out and conceals the universe is living in an air-castle.

The man who believes that all humanity is united in conspiracy against him, who feels that his life is the hardest in all the world, and lets the cares, sorrows and trials that come to us all, eclipse the glorious sun of his happiness, darkening his eyes to his privileges and his blessings, is living in an air-castle.

The woman who thinks the most beautiful creature in the world is seen in her mirror, and who exchanges her queenly heritage of noble living for the shams, jealousies, follies, frivolities and pretences of society, is living in an air-castle.

The man who makes wealth his god instead of his servant, who is determined to get rich, rich at any cost, and who is willing to sacrifice honesty, honor, loyalty, character, family—everything he should hold dear—for the sake of a mere stack of money-bags, is, despite his robes of ermine, only a rich pauper living in an air-castle.

The man of ultra-conservatism, the victim of false content, who has no plans, no ideals, no aspirations beyond the dull round of daily duties in which he moves like a gold-fish in a globe, is often vain enough to boast of his lack of progressiveness, in cheap shop-worn phrases from those whom he permits to do his thinking for him. He does not realize that faithfulness to duties, in its highest sense, means the constant aiming at the performance of higher duties, living up, so far as can be, to the maximum of one's possibilities, not resignedly plodding along at the minimum. A piece of machinery will do this, but real men ever seek to rise to higher uses. Such a man is living in an air-castle.

With patronizing contempt he scorns the man of earnest, thoughtful purpose, who sees his goal far before him but is willing to pay any honest price to attain it; content to work day by day unceasingly, through storm and stress, and sunshine and shadow, with sublime confidence that nature is storing up every stroke of his effort, that, though times often seem dark and progress but slight, results must come if he have but courage to fight bravely to the end. This man does not live in an air-castle; he is but battling with destiny for the possession of his heritage, and is strengthened in character by his struggle, even though all that he desires may not be fully awarded him.

The man who permits regret for past misdeeds, or sorrow for lost opportunities to keep him from recreating a proud future from the new days committed to his care, is losing much of the glory of living. He is repudiating the manna of new life given each new day, merely because he misused the manna of years ago. He is doubly unwise, because he has the wisdom of his past experience and does not profit by it, merely because of a technicality of useless, morbid regret. He is living in an air-castle.

The man who spends his time lamenting the fortune he once had, or the fame that has taken its winged flight into oblivion, frittering away his golden hours erecting new monuments in the cemetery of his past achievements and his former greatness, making what he was ever plead apology for what he is, lives in an air-castle. To the world and to the individual a single egg of new hope and determination, with its wondrous potency of new life, is greater than a thousand nests full of the eggs of dead dreams, or unrealized ambitions.

Whatever keeps a man from living his best, truest and highest life now, in the indicative present, if it be something that he himself places as an obstacle in his own path of progress and development, is to him an air-castle.

Some men live in the air-castle of indolence; others in the air-castle of dissipation, of pride, of avarice, of deception, of bigotry, of worry, of intemperance, of injustice, of intolerance, of procrastination, of lying, of selfishness, or of some other mental or moral characteristic that withdraws them from the real duties and privileges of living.

Let us find out what is the air-castle in which we, individually, spend most of our time and we can then begin a re-creation of ourselves. The bondage of the air-castle must be fought nobly and untiringly.

As man spends his hours and his days and his weeks in an air-castle, he finds that the delicate gossamer-like strands and lines of the phantom structure gradually become less and less airy; they begin to grow firm and firmer, strengthening with the years, until at last, solid walls hem him in. Then he is startled by the awful realization that habit and habitancy have transformed his air-castle into a prison from which escape is difficult.

And then he learns that the most deceptive and dangerous of all things is,—the air-castle.

4. Swords and Scabbards

It is the custom of grateful states and nations to present swords as tokens of highest honor to the victorious leaders of their armies and navies. The sword presented to Admiral Schley by the people of Philadelphia, at the close of America's war with Spain, cost over $3,500, the greater part of which was spent on the jewels and decorations on the scabbard. A little more than half a century ago, when General Winfield Scott, for whom Admiral Schley was named, received a beautiful sword from the State of Louisiana, he was asked how it pleased him.

"It is a very fine sword, indeed," he said, "but there is one thing about it I would have preferred different. The inscription should be on the blade, not on the scabbard. The scabbard may be taken from us; the sword, never."

The world spends too much time, money and energy on the scabbard of life; too little on the sword. The scabbard represents outside show, vanity and display; the sword, intrinsic worth. The scabbard is ever the semblance; the sword the reality. The scabbard is the temporal; the sword is the eternal. The scabbard is the body; the sword is the soul. The scabbard typifies the material side of life; the sword the true, the spiritual, the ideal.

The man who does not dare follow his own convictions, but who lives in terror of what society will say, falling prostrate before the golden calf of public opinion, is living an empty life of mere show. He is sacrificing his individuality, his divine right to live his life in harmony with his own high ideals, to a cowardly, toadying fear of the world. He is not a voice, with the strong note of individual purpose; he is but the thin echo of the voice of thousands. He is not brightening, sharpening and using the sword of his life in true warfare; he is lazily ornamenting a useless scabbard with the hieroglyphics of his folly.

The man who lives beyond his means, who mortgages his future for his present, who is generous before he is just, who is sacrificing everything to keep up with the procession of his superiors, is really losing much of life. He, too, is decorating the scabbard, and letting the sword rust in its sheath.

Life is not a competition with others. In its truest sense it is rivalry with ourselves. We should each day seek to break the record of our yesterday. We should seek each day to live stronger, better, truer lives; each day to master some weakness of yesterday; each day to repair past follies; each day to surpass ourselves. And this is but progress. And individual, conscious progress, progress unending and unlimited, is the one great thing that differentiates man from all the other animals. Then we will care naught for the pretty, useless decorations of society's approval on the scabbard. For us it will be enough to know that the blade of our purpose is kept ever keen and sharp for the defense of right and truth, never to wrong the rights of others, but ever to right the wrongs of ourselves and those around us.

Reputation is what the world thinks a man is; character is what he really is. Anyone can play shuttlecock with a man's reputation; his character is his alone. No one can injure his character but he himself. Character is the sword; reputation is the scabbard. Many men acquire insomnia in standing guard over their reputation, while their character gives them no concern. Often they make new dents in their character in their attempt to cut a deep, deceptive filigree on the scabbard of their reputation. Reputation is the shell a man discards when he leaves life for immortality. His character he takes with him.

The woman who spends thousands in charitable donations, and is hard and uncharitable in her judgments, sentimentally sympathetic with human sin and weakness in the abstract, while she arrogates to herself omniscience in her harsh condemnation of individual lapses, is charitable only on the outside. She is letting her tongue undo the good work of her hand. She is too enthusiastic in decorating the scabbard of publicity to think of the sword of real love of humanity.

He who carries avarice to the point of becoming a miser, hoarding gold that is made useless to him because it does not fulfill its one function, circulation, and regarding the necessities of life as luxuries, is one of Nature's jests, that would be humorous were it not so serious. He is the most difficult animal to classify in the whole natural history of humanity—he has so many of the virtues. He is a striking example of ambition, economy, frugality, persistence, will-power, self-denial, loyalty to purpose and generosity to his heirs. These noble qualities he spoils in the application. His specialty is the scabbard of life. He spends his days in making a solid gold scabbard for the tin sword of a wasted existence.

The shoddy airs and ostentations, extravagance, and prodigality of some who have suddenly become rich, is goldplating the scabbard without improving the blade. The superficial veneer of refinement really accentuates the native vulgarity. The more you polish woodwork, the more you reveal the grain. Some of the sudden legatees of fortune have the wisdom to acquire the reality of refinement through careful training. This is the true method of putting the sword itself in order instead of begemming the scabbard.

The girl who marries merely for money or for a title, is a feminine Esau of the beginning of the century. She is selling her birthright of love for the pottage of an empty name, forfeiting the possibility of a life of love, all that true womanhood should hold most dear, for a mere bag of gold or a crown. She is decorating the scabbard with a crest and heraldic designs, and with ornaments of pure gold set with jewels. She feels that this will be enough for life, and that she does not need love,—real love, that has made this world a paradise, despite all the other people present. She does not realize that there is but one real reason, but one justification for marriage, and that is,—love; all the other motives are not reasons, they are only excuses. The phrase, "marrying a man for his money," as the world bluntly puts it, is incorrect—the woman merely marries the money, and takes the man as an incumbrance or mortgage on the property.

The man who procrastinates, filling his ears with the lovely song of "to-morrow," is following the easiest and most restful method of shortening the possibilities of life. Procrastination is stifling action by delay, it is killing decision by inactivity, it is drifting on the river of time, instead of rowing bravely toward a desired harbor. It is watching the sands in the hour-glass run down before beginning any new work, then reversing the glass and repeating the observation. The folly of man in thus delaying is apparent, when any second his life may stop, and the sands of that single hour may run their course,—and he will not be there to see.

Delay is the narcotic that paralyzes energy. When Alexander was asked how he conquered the world, he said: "By not delaying." Let us not put off till to-morrow the duty of to-day; that which our mind tells us should be done to-day, our mind and body should execute. To-day is the sword we should hold and use; to-morrow is but the scabbard from which each new to-day is withdrawn.

The man who wears an oppressive, pompous air of dignity, because he has accomplished some little work of importance, because he is vested with a brief mantle of authority, loses sight of the true perspective of life. He is destitute of humor; he takes himself seriously. It is a thousand-dollar scabbard on a two-dollar sword.

The man who is guilty of envy is the victim of the oldest vice in the history of the world, the meanest and most despicable of human traits. It began in the Garden of Eden, when Satan envied Adam and Eve. It caused the downfall of man and the first murder— Cain's unbrotherly act to Abel. Envy is a paradoxic vice. It cannot suffer bravely the prosperity of another, it has mental dyspepsia because someone else is feasting, it makes its owner's clothes turn into rags at sight of another's velvet. Envy is the malicious contemplation of the beauty, honors, success, happiness, or triumph of another. It is the mud that inferiority throws at success. Envy is the gangrene of unsatisfied ambition, it eats away purpose and kills energy. It is egotism gone to seed; it always finds the secret of its non-success in something outside itself.

Envy is the scabbard, but emulation is the sword. Emulation regards the success of another as an object lesson; it seeks in the triumph of another the why, the reason, the inspiration of method. It seeks to attain the same heights by the path it thus discovers, not to hurl down from his eminence him who points out the way of attainment. Let us keep the sword of emulation ever brightened and sharpened in the battle of honest effort, not idly dulling and rusting in the scabbard of envy.

The supreme folly of the world, the saddest depths to which the human mind can sink, is atheism. He surely is to be pitied who permits the illogical philosophy of petty infidels, or his misinterpretations of the revelations of science, to cheat him of his God. He pins his faith to some ingenious sophistry in the reasoning of those whose books he has read to sum up for him the whole problem, and in hopeless egotism shuts his eyes to the million proofs in nature and life, because the full plans of Omnipotence are not made clear to him.

On the technicality of his failure to understand some one point—perhaps it is why sin, sorrow, suffering and injustice exist in the world—he declares he will not believe. He might as well disbelieve in the sky above him because he cannot see it all; discredit the air he breathes because it is invisible; doubt the reality of the ocean because his feeble vision can take in but a few miles of the great sea; deny even life itself because he cannot see it, and no anatomist has found the subtle essence to hold it up to view on the end of his scalpel.

He dares to disbelieve in God despite His countless manifestations, because he is not taken into the full confidence of the Creator and permitted to look over and check off the ground-plans of the universe. He sheathes the sword of belief in the dingy scabbard of infidelity. He does not see the proof of God in the daily miracle of the rising and setting of the sun, in the seasons, in the birds, in the flowers, in the countless stars, moving in their majestic regularity at the command of eternal law, in the presence of love, justice, truth in the hearts of men, in that supreme confidence that is inborn in humanity, making even the lowest savage worship the Infinite in some form. It is the petty vanity of cheap reasoning that makes man permit the misfit scabbard of infidelity to hide from him the glory of the sword of belief.

The philosophy of swords and scabbards is as true of nations as of individuals. When France committed the great crime of the nineteenth century, by condemning Dreyfus to infamy and isolation, deafening her ears to the cries of justice, and seeking to cover her shame with greater shame, she sheathed the sword of a nation's honor in the scabbard of a nation's crime. The breaking of the sword of Dreyfus when he was cruelly degraded before the army, typified the degradation of the French nation in breaking the sword of justice and preserving carefully the empty scabbard with its ironic inscription, "Vive la justice."

The scabbard is ever useless in the hour of emergency; then it is upon the sword itself that we must rely. Then the worthlessness of show, sham, pretence, gilded weakness is revealed to us. Then the trivialities of life are seen in their true form. The nothingness of everything but the real, the tried, the true, is made luminant in an instant. Then we know whether our living has been one of true preparation, of keeping the sword clean, pure, sharp and ready, or one of mere idle, meaningless, day-by-day markings of folly on the empty scabbard of a wasted life.

5. The Conquest of the Preventable

This world would be a delightful place to live in—if it were not for the people. They really cause all the trouble. Man's worst enemy is always man. He began to throw the responsibility of his transgressions on some one else in the Garden of Eden, and he has been doing so ever since.

The greater part of the pain, sorrow and misery in life is purely a human invention, yet man, with cowardly irreverence, dares to throw the responsibility on God. It comes through breaking laws, laws natural, physical, civic, mental or moral. These are laws which man knows, but he disregards; he takes chances; he thinks he can dodge results in some way. But Nature says, "He who breaks, pays." There are no dead-letter laws on the divine statute-books of life. When a man permits a torchlight procession to parade through a powder magazine, it is not courteous for him to refer to the subsequent explosion as "one of the mysterious workings of Providence."

Nine tenths of the world's sorrow, misfortune and unhappiness is preventable. The daily newspapers are the great chroniclers of the dominance of the unnecessary. Paragraph after paragraph, column after column, and page after page of the dark story—accidents, disasters, crime, scandal, human weakness and sin—might be checked off with the word "preventable." In each instance were our information full enough, our analysis keen enough, we could trace each back to its cause, to the weakness or the wrong from which it emanated. Sometimes it is carelessness, inattention, neglect of duty, avarice, anger, jealousy, dissipation, betrayal of trust, selfishness, hypocrisy, revenge, dishonesty,—any of a hundred phases of the preventable.

That which can be prevented, should be prevented. It all rests with the individual. The "preventable" exists in three degrees: First, that which is due to the individual solely and directly; second, that which he suffers through the wrong-doing of those around him, other individuals; third, those instances wherein he is the unnecessary victim of the wrongs of society, the innocent legatee of the folly of humanity—and society is but the massing of thousands of individuals with the heritage of manners, customs and laws they have received from the past.

We sometimes feel heart-sick and weary in facing failure, when the fortune that seemed almost in our fingers slips away because of the envy, malice or treachery of some one else. We bow under the weight of a sorrow that makes all life grow dark and the star of hope fade from our vision; or we meet some unnecessary misfortune with a dumb, helpless despair. "It is all wrong," we say, "it is cruel, it is unjust. Why is it permitted?" And, in the very intensity of our feeling, we half-unconsciously repeat the words over and over again, in monotonous iteration, as if in some way the very repetition might bring relief, might somehow soothe us. Yet, in most instances, it could be prevented. No suffering is caused in the world by right. Whatever sorrow there is that is preventable, comes from inharmony or wrong of some kind.

In the divine economy of the universe most of the evil, pain and suffering are unnecessary, even when overruled for good, and perhaps, if our knowledge were perfect, it would be seen that none is necessary, that all is preventable. The fault is mine, or yours, or the fault of the world. It is always individual. The world itself is but the cohesive united force of the thoughts, words and deeds of millions who have lived or who are living, like you and me. By individuals has the great wrong that causes our preventable sorrow been built up, by individuals must it be weakened and transformed to right. And in this, too, it is to a great degree our fault; we care so little about rousing public sentiment, of lashing it into activity unless it concerns us individually.

The old Greek fable of Atlas, the African king, who supported the world on his shoulders, has a modern application. The individual is the Atlas upon whom the fate of the world rests to-day. Let each individual do his best,—and the result is foreordained; it is but a matter of the unconquerable massing of the units. Let each individual bear his part as faithfully as though all the responsibility rested on him, yet as calmly, as gently and as unworried as though all the responsibility rested on others.

Most accidents are preventable—as at Balaclava, "someone has blundered." One of the great disasters of the nineteenth century was the Johnstown flood, where the bursting of a dam caused the loss of more than six thousand lives. The flood was not a mere accident, it was a crime. A leaking dam, for more than a year known to be unsafe, known to be unable to withstand any increased pressure, stood at the head of the valley. Below it lay a chain of villages containing over forty-five thousand persons in the direct line of the flood. When the heavy rains came the weakened dam gave way. Had there been one individual, one member of the South Fork Fishing Club brave enough to have done merely his duty, one member with the courage to so move his fellows and to stir up public action to make the barrier safe, over six thousand murders could have been prevented.

When a tired engineer, sleepy from overwork, can no longer cheat nature of her needed rest, and, drowsing for a moment in his cab, fails to see the red signal light of danger, or to heed the exploding of the warning torpedo, the wreck that follows is not chargeable to the Almighty. It is but an awful memorial of a railroad corporation's struggle to save two dollars. One ounce of prevention is worth six pounds of coroner's inquest. It is a crime to balance the safety and sacredness of human life in the scales with the petty saving that comes from transforming a man into a mechanism and forgetting he has either a soul or a body. True, just and wise labor laws are part of society's weapon for fighting the preventable.

When a terrible fire makes a city desolate and a nation mourn, the investigation that follows usually shows that a little human foresight could have prevented it, or at least, lessened the horror of it all. If chemicals or dynamite are stored in any building in excess of what wise legislation declares is safe, some one has been cruelly careless. Perhaps it is some inspector who has been disloyal to his trust, by permitting bribes to chloroform his sense of duty. If the lack of fire-escapes adds its quota to the list of deaths, or if the avarice of the owner has made his building a fire-trap, public feeling becomes intense, the newspapers are justly loud in their protests, and in demands that the guilty ones be punished. "If the laws already on the statute books do not cover the situation," we hear from day to day, "new laws will be framed to make a repetition of the tragedy impossible"; we are promised all kinds of reforms; the air seems filled with a spirit of regeneration; the mercury of public indignation rises to the point where "fever-heat" seems a mild, inadequate term.

Then, as the horror begins to fade in the perspective of the past, men go quietly back to their own personal cares and duties, and the mighty wave of righteous protest that threatened so much, dies in gentle lapping on the shore. What has been all men's concern seems soon to concern no one. The tremendous energy of the authorities seems like the gesture of a drunken man, that starts from his shoulder with a force that would almost fell an ox but when it reaches the hand it has expended itself, and the hand drops listlessly in the air with hardly power enough to disturb the serenity of a butterfly. There is always a little progress, a slight advance, and it is only the constant accumulation of these steps that is giving to the world greater dominion over the preventable.

Constant vigilance is the price of the conquest of the preventable. We have no right to admit any wrong or evil in the world as necessary, until we have exhausted every precaution that human wisdom can suggest to prevent it. When a man with a pistol in his right hand, clumsily covered with a suspicious-looking handkerchief, moved along in a line of people, and presenting his left hand to President McKinley, pressed his weapon to the breast of the Chief Executive of the American people, some one of the secret service men, paid by the nation to guard their ruler, should have watched so zealously that the tragedy would have been impossible. Two Presidents had already been sacrificed, but twenty years of immunity had brought a dreamy sense of security that lessened the vigilance. We should emulate the example of the insurance companies who decline certain risks that are "extra hazardous."

Poverty has no necessary place in life. It is a disease that results from the weakness, sin, and selfishness of humanity. Nature is boundless in her generosity; the world produces sufficient to give food, clothing, and comfort to every individual. Poverty is preventable. Poverty may result from the shiftlessness, idleness, intemperance, improvidence, lack of purpose or evil-doing of the individual himself.

If the causes do not exist in the individual, they may be found in the second class, in the wrong-doing of those around him, in the oppression of labor by capital, in the grinding process by which corporations seek to crush the individual. The individual may be the victim of any of a thousand phases of the wrong of others. The poverty caused by the third class, the weakness and injustice of human laws and human institutions, is also preventable, but to reach the cause requires time and united heroic effort of all individuals.

In the battle against poverty, those writers who seek to inflame the poor against the rich, to foment discontent between labor and capital, do grievous wrong to both. What the world needs is to have the two brought closer together in the bonds of human brotherhood. The poor should learn more of the cares, responsibilities, unrecorded charities, and absorbing worries of the rich; the rich should learn more intimately the sorrows, privations, struggles, and despair of poverty.

The world is learning the great truth, that the best way to prevent crime is to study the sociologic conditions in which it flourishes, to seek to give each man a better chance of living his real life by removing, if possible, the elements that make wrong easy, and to him, almost necessary, and by inspiring him to fight life's battle bravely with all the help others can give him. Science is coöperating with religion in striving to conquer the evil at the root instead of the evil manifest as crime in the fruit of the branches. It is so much wiser to prevent than to cure; to keep some one from being burned is so much better than inventing new poultices for unnecessary hurts.

It is ever the little things that make up the sum of human misery. All the wild animals of the world combined do but trifling damage, when compared with the ravages of insect pests. The crimes of humanity, the sins that make us start back affrighted, do not cause as much sorrow and unhappiness in life as the multitude of little sins, of omission and commission, that the individual, and millions like him, must meet every day. They are not the evil deeds that the law can reach or punish, they are but the infinity of petty wrongs for which man can never be tried until he stands with bowed head before the bar of justice of his own conscience.

The bitter words of anger and reproach that rise so easily to our lips and give us a moment's fleeting satisfaction in thus venting our feelings, may change the current of the whole life of some one near to us. The thoughtless speech, revealing our lack of tact and sympathy, cannot be recalled and made nothing by the plea, "I didn't think." To sensitive souls this is no justification; they feel that our hearts should be so filled with the instinct of love that our lips would need no tutor or guardian.

Our unfulfilled duty may bring unhappiness and misery to hundreds. The dressmaker's bill that a rich woman may toss lightly aside, as being an affair of no moment, to be settled at her serene pleasure, may bring sorrow, privation or even failure to her debtor, and through her to a long chain of others. The result, if seen in all its stern reality, seems out of all proportion to the cause. There are places in the Alps, where great masses of snow are so lightly poised that even the report of a gun might start a vibration that would dislodge an avalanche, and send it on its death-mission into the valley.

The individual who would live his life to the best that is within him must make each moment one of influence for good. He must set before him as one of his ideals, to be progressively realized in each day of his living: "If I cannot accomplish great deeds in the world, I will do all the good I can by the faithful performance of the duties that come to my hand and being ever ready for all opportunities. And I will consecrate myself to the conquest of the preventable."

Let the individual say each day, as he rises new-created to face a new life: "To-day no one in the world shall suffer because I live. I will be kind, considerate, careful in thought and speech and act. I will seek to discover the element that weakens me as a power in the world, and that keeps me from living up to the fullness of my possibility. That weakness I will master to-day. I will conquer it, at any cost."

When any failure or sorrow comes to the individual, he should be glad if he can prove to himself that it was his fault,—for then he has the remedy in his own hands. Lying, intrigue, jealousy are never remedies that can prevent an evil. They postpone it, merely to augment it. They are merely deferring payment of a debt which has to be met later,—with compound interest. It is like trying to put out a fire by pouring kerosene on the flames.

Jealousy in the beginning is but a thought,—in the end it may mean the gallows. Selfishness often assumes seemingly harmless guises, yet it is the foundation of the world's unhappiness. Disloyalty may seem to be a rare quality, but society is saturated with it. Judas acquired his reputation because of his proficiency in it. Sympathy which should be the atmosphere of every individual life is as rare as human charity. The world is suffering from an over-supply of unnecessary evils, created by man. They should be made luxuries, then man could dispense with them.

The world needs societies formed of members pledged to the individual conquest of preventable pain and sorrow. The individual has no right that runs counter to the right of any one else. There are no solo parts in the eternal music of life. Each must pour out his life in duo with every other. Every moment must be one of choice, of good or of evil. Which will the individual choose? His life will be his answer. Let him dedicate his life to making the world around him brighter, sweeter and better, and by his conquest of preventable pain and sorrow he will day by day get fuller revelation of the glory of the possibilities of individual living, and come nearer and nearer to the realization of his ideals.

6. The Companionship of Tolerance

Intolerance is part of the unnecessary friction of life. It is prejudice on the war-path. Intolerance acknowledges only one side of any question,—its own. It is the assumption of a monopoly in thinking, the attitude of the man who believes he has a corner on wisdom and truth, in some phase of life.

Tolerance is a calm, generous respect for the opinions of others, even of one's enemies. It recognizes the right of every man to think his own thoughts, to live his own life, to be himself in all things, so long as he does not run counter to the rights of others. It means giving to others the same freedom that we ourselves crave. Tolerance is silent justice, blended with sympathy. If he who is tolerant desires to show to others the truth as he sees it, he seeks with gentleness and deference to point out the way in which he has found peace, and certainty, and rest; he tries to raise them to the recognition of higher ideals, as he has found them inspiring; he endeavors in a spirit of love and comradeship with humanity to lead others rather than to drive them, to persuade and convince rather than to overawe and eclipse.

Tolerance does not use the battering-ram of argument or the club of sarcasm, or the rapier of ridicule, in discussing the weakness or wrongs of individuals. It may lash or scourge the evil of an age, but it is kind and tender with the individual; it may flay the sin, but not the sinner. Tolerance makes the individual regard truth as higher than personal opinion; it teaches him to live with the windows of his life open towards the east to catch the first rays of the sunlight of truth no matter from whom it comes, and to realize that the faith that he so harshly condemns may have the truth he desires if he would only look into it and test it before he repudiates it so cavalierly.

This world of ours is growing better, more tolerant and liberal. The days when difference in political opinions was solved and cured by the axe and the block; when a man's courage to stand by his religion meant facing the horrors of the Inquisition or the cruelty of the stake, when daring to think their own thoughts on questions of science brought noble men to a pallet of straw and a dungeon cell,—these days have, happily, passed away. Intolerance and its twin brother, Ignorance, weaken and die when the pure white light of wisdom is thrown upon them. Knowledge is the death-knell of intolerance—not mere book-learning, nor education in schools or colleges, nor accumulation of mere statistics, nor shreds of information, but the large sympathetic study of the lives, manners, customs, aims, thoughts, struggles, progress, motives and ideals of other ages, other nations, other individuals.

Tolerance unites men in the closer bonds of human brotherhood, brings them together in unity and sympathy in essentials and gives them greater liberality and freedom in non-essentials. Napoleon when First Consul said, "Let there be no more Jacobins, nor Moderates, nor Royalists: let all be Frenchmen." Sectionalism and sectarianism always mean concentration on the body of a part at the expense of the soul of the whole. The religious world to-day needs more Christ and less sects in its gospel. When Christ lived on earth Christianity was a unit; when he died sects began.

There are in America to-day, hundreds of small towns, scattered over the face of the land, that are over-supplied with churches. In many of these towns, just emerging from the short dresses of village-hood, there are a dozen or more weak churches, struggling to keep their organization alive. Between these churches there is often only a slight difference in creed, the tissue-paper wall of some technicality of belief. Half-starved, dragging out a mere existence, trying to fight a large mortgage with a small congregation and a small contribution box, there is little spiritual fervor. By combination, by coöperation, by tolerance, by the mutual surrender of non-essentials and a strong, vital concentration and unity on the great fundamental realities of Christianity, their spiritual health and possibilities could be marvellously increased. Three or four sturdy, live, growing churches would then take the place of a dozen strugglers. Why have a dozen weak bridges across a stream, if greater good can come from three or four stronger ones, or even a single strongest bridge? The world needs a great religious trust which will unite the churches into a single body of faith, to precede and prepare the way for the greater religious trust, predicted in Holy Writ,—the millennium.

We can ever be loyal to our own belief, faithful to our own cause, without condemning those who give their fidelity in accord with their own conscience or desires. The great reformers of the world, men who are honestly and earnestly seeking to solve the great social problems and to provide means for meeting human sin and wrong, agreeing perfectly in their estimate of the gravity and awfulness of the situation, often propose diametrically opposite methods. They are regarding the subject from different points of view, and it would be intolerance for us, who are looking on, to condemn the men on either side merely because we cannot accept their verdict as our own.

On the great national questions brought before statesmen for their decision, men equally able, equally sincere, just and unselfish, differ in their remedies. One, as a surgeon, suggests cutting away the offending matter, the use of the knife,—this typifies the sword, or war. Another, as a doctor, urges medicine that will absorb and cure,—this is the prescription of the diplomat. The third suggests waiting for developments, leaving the case with time and nature,—this is the conservative. But all three classes agree as to the evil and the need of meeting it.

The conflict of authorities on every great question to be settled by human judgment should make us tolerant of the opinion of others, though we may be as confident of the rightness of the judgment we have formed as if it were foreordained from the day of the creation. But if we receive any new light that makes us see clearer, let us change at once without that foolish consistency of some natures that continue to use last year's almanac as a guide to this year's eclipses. Tolerance is ever progressive.

Intolerance believes it is born with the peculiar talent for managing the affairs of others, without any knowledge of the details, better than the men themselves, who are giving their life's thought to the vital questions. Intolerance is the voice of the Pharisee still crying through the ages and proclaiming his infallibility.

Let us not seek to fit the whole world with shoes from our individual last. If we think that all music ceased to be written when Wagner laid down the pen, let us not condemn those who find enjoyment in light opera. Perhaps they may sometime rise to our heights of artistic appreciation and learn the proper parts to applaud. If their lighter music satisfies their souls, is our Wagner doing more for us? It is not fair to take from a child its rag doll in order to raise it to the appreciation of the Venus de Milo. The rag doll is its Venus; it may require a long series of increasingly better dolls to lead it to realize the beauties of the marble woman of Melos.

Intolerance makes its great mistakes in measuring the needs of others from its own standpoint. Intolerance ignores the personal equation in life. What would be an excellent book for a man of forty might be worse than useless for a boy of thirteen. The line of activity in life that we would choose as our highest dream of bliss, as our Paradise, might, if forced on another, be to him worse than the after-death fate of the wicked, according to the old-fashioned theologians. What would be a very acceptable breakfast for a sparrow would be a very poor meal for an elephant.

When we sit in solemn judgment of the acts and characters of those around us and condemn them with the easy nonchalance of our ignorance, yet with the assumption of omniscience we reveal our intolerance. Tolerance ever leads us to recognize and respect the differences in the natures of those who are near to us, to make allowance for differences in training, in opportunities, in ideals, in motives, in tastes, in opinions, in temperaments and in feelings. Intolerance seeks to live other people's lives for them; sympathy helps us to live their lives with them. We must accept humanity with all its weakness, sin and folly and seek to make the best of it, just as humanity must accept us. We learn this lesson as we grow older, and, with the increase of our knowledge of the world, we see how much happier life would have been for us and for others if we had been more tolerant, more charitable, more generous.

No one in the world is absolutely perfect; if he were he would probably be translated from earth to heaven, as was Elijah of old, without waiting for the sprouting of wings or the passport of death. It is a hard lesson for youth to learn, but we must realize, as the old college professor said to his class of students, bowed with the consciousness of their wisdom: "No one of us is infallible, no, not even the youngest." Let us accept the little failings of those around us as we accept facts in nature, and make the best of them, as we accept the hard shells of nuts, the skin of fruits, the shadow that always accompanies light. These are not absolute faults, they are often but individual peculiarities. Intolerance sees the mote in its neighbor's eye as larger than the beam in its own.

Instead of concentrating our thought on the one weak spot in a character, let us seek to find some good quality that offsets it, just as a credit may more than cancel a debt on a ledger account. Let us not constantly speak of roses having thorns, let us be thankful that the thorns have roses. In Nature there are both thorns and prickles; thorns are organic, they have their root deep in the fibre and the being of the twig; prickles are superficial, they are lightly held in the cuticle or covering of the twig. There are thorns in character that reveal an internal inharmony, that can be controlled only from within; there are also prickles, which are merely peculiarities of temperament, that the eye of tolerance may overlook and the finger of charity can gently remove.

The tenderness of tolerance will illuminate and glorify the world,—as moonlight makes all things beautiful,—if we only permit it. Measuring a man by his weakness alone is unjust. This little frailty may be but a small mortgage on a large estate, and it is narrow and petty to judge by the mortgage on a character. Let us consider the "equity," the excess of the real value over the claim against it.

Unless we sympathetically seek to discover the motive behind the act, to see the circumstances that inspired a course of living, the target at which a man is aiming, our snap condemnations are but arrogant and egotistic expressions of our intolerance. All things must be studied relatively instead of absolutely. The hour hand on a clock does just as valuable work as the minute hand, even though it is shorter and seems to do only one-twelfth as much.

Intolerance in the home circle shows itself in overdiscipline, in an atmosphere of severity heavy with prohibitions. The home becomes a place strewn with "Please keep off the grass" signs. It means the suppression of individuality, the breaking of the wills of children, instead of their development and direction. It is the foolish attempt to mould them from the outside, as a potter does clay; the higher conception is the wise training that helps the child to help himself in his own growth. Parents often forget their own youth; they do not sympathize with their children in their need of pleasure, of dress, of companionship. There should be a few absolutely firm rules on essentials, the basic principles of living, with the largest possible leeway for the varying manifestations of individuality in unimportant phases. Confidence, sympathy, love and trust would generate a spirit of tolerance and sweetness that would work marvels. Intolerance converts live, natural children into prigs of counterfeit virtue and irritatingly good automatons of obedience.

Tolerance is a state of mutual concessions. In the family life there should be this constant reciprocity of independence, this mutual forbearance. It is the instinctive recognition of the sacredness of individuality, the right of each to live his own life as best he can. When we set ourselves up as dictators to tyrannize over the thoughts, words and acts of others, we are sacrificing the kingly power of influence with which we may help others, for the petty triumph of tyranny which repels and loses them.

Perhaps one reason why the sons of great and good men so often go astray is that the earnestness, strength and virtue of the father, exacting strict obedience to the letter of the law, kills the appreciation of the spirit of it, breeding an intolerance that forces submission under which the fire of protest and rebellion is smouldering, ready to burst into flame at the first breath of freedom. Between brother and sister, husband and wife, parent and child, master and servant, the spirit of tolerance, of "making allowances," transforms a house of gloom and harshness into a home of sweetness and love.

In the sacred relation of parent to child there always comes a time when the boy becomes a man, when she whom the father still regards but as a little girl faces the great problems of life as an individual. The coming of years of discretion brings a day when the parents must surrender their powers of trusteeship, when the individual enters upon his heritage of freedom and responsibility. Parents have still the right and privilege of counsel and of helpful, loving insight their children should respect. But in meeting a great question, when the son or daughter stands before a problem that means happiness or misery for a lifetime, it must be for him or for her to decide. Coercion, bribery, undue influence, threats of disinheritance, and the other familiar weapons, are cruel, selfish, arrogant and unjust. A child is a human being, free to make his own life, not a slave. There is a clearly marked dead-line that it is intolerance to cross.

Let us realize that tolerance is ever broadening; it develops sympathy, weakens worry and inspires calmness. It is but charity and optimism, it is Christianity as a living eternal fact, not a mere theory. Let us be tolerant of the weakness of others, sternly intolerant of our own. Let us seek to forgive and forget the faults of others, losing sight, to a degree, of what they are in the thought of what they may become. Let us fill their souls with the inspiring revelation of their possibilities in the majestic evolution march of humanity. Let us see, for ourselves and for them, in the acorn of their present the towering oak of their future.

We should realize the right of every human soul to work out its own destiny, with our aid, our sympathy, our inspiration, if we are thus privileged to help him to live his life; but it is intolerance to try to live it for him. He sits alone on the throne of his individuality; he must reign alone, and at the close of his rule must give his own account to the God of the ages of the deeds of his kingship. Life is a dignified privilege, a glorious prerogative of every man, and it is arrogant intolerance that touches the sacred ark with the hand of unkind condemnation.

7. The Things that Come too Late

Time seems a grim old humorist, with a fondness for afterthoughts. The things that come too late are part of his sarcasm. Each generation is engaged in correcting the errors of its predecessors, and in supplying new blunders for its own posterity to set right. Each generation bequeaths to its successor its wisdom and its folly, its wealth of knowledge and its debts of error and failure. The things that come too late thus mean only the delayed payments on old debts. They mean that the world is growing wiser, and better, truer, nobler, and more just. It is emerging from the dark shadows of error into the sunshine of truth and justice. They prove that Time is weaving a beauteous fabric from the warp and woof of humanity, made up of shreds and tangles of error and truth.

The things that come too late are the fuller wisdom, the deferred honors, the truer conception of the work of pioneers, the brave sturdy fighters who battled alone for truth and were misunderstood and unrecognized. It means the world's finer attitude toward life. If looked at superficially, the things that come too late make us feel helpless, hopeless, pessimistic; if seen with the eye of deeper wisdom, they reveal to us the grand evolution march of humanity toward higher things. It is Nature's proclamation that, in the end, Right must triumph, Truth must conquer, and Justice must reign. For us, as individuals, it is a warning and an inspiration,—a warning against withholding love, charity, kindness, sympathy, justice, and helpfulness, till it is too late; an inspiration for us to live ever at our best, ever up to the maximum of effort, not worrying about results, but serenely confident that they must come.

It takes over thirty years for the light of some of the stars to reach the earth, some a hundred, some a thousand years. Those stars do not become visible till their light reaches and reacts on human vision. It takes an almost equal time for the light of some of the world's great geniuses to meet real, seeing eyes. Then we see these men as the brilliant stars in the world's gallery of immortal great ones. This is why contemporary reputation rarely indicates lasting fame. We are constantly mistaking fireflies of cleverness for stars of genius. But Time brings all things right. The fame, though, brings no joy, or encouragement, or inspiration to him who has passed beyond this world's lights and shadows; it has the sadness of the honors that come too late, a touch of the farcical mingled with its pathos. Tardy recognition is better than none at all, it is better, though late, than never; but it is so much truer and kinder and more valuable if never late. We are so inclined to send our condemnation and our snapshot criticisms by express, and our careful, honest commendation by slow freight.

In October, 1635, Roger Williams, because of his inspiring pleas for individual liberty, was ordered by the General Court of Massachusetts to leave the colony forever. He went to Rhode Island, where he lived for nearly fifty years. But the official conscience grew a little restless, and a few years ago, in April, 1899, Massachusetts actually made atonement for its rash act. The original papers, yellow, faded, and crumbling, were taken from their pigeonhole tomb, and "by an ordinary motion, made, seconded, and adopted," the order of banishment was solemnly "annulled and repealed, and made of no effect whatever." The ban, under which Roger Williams had lain for over 260 years, was lifted. And there is no reason now, according to law, why Roger Williams cannot enter the State of Massachusetts and reside therein. The action was to the credit and honor of the State; it was right in its spirit, and Roger being in the spirit for more than two centuries, may have smiled gently and understood. But the reparation was really—over-delayed.

The mistakes, the sin and folly of one age may be partially atoned for by a succeeding age, but the individual stands alone. For what we do and for what we leave undone, we alone are responsible. If we permit the golden hours that might be consecrated to higher things to trickle like sand through our fingers, no one can ever restore them to us.

Human affection is fed by signs and tokens of that affection. Merely having kindly feelings is not enough, they should be made manifest in action. The parched earth is not refreshed by the mere fact of water in the clouds, it is only when the blessing of rain actually descends that it awakens to new life. We are so ready to say "He knows how much I think of him," and to assume that as a fitting substitute for expression. We may know that the sun is shining somewhere and still shiver for lack of its glow and warmth. Love should be constantly made evident in little acts of thoughtfulness, words of sweetness and appreciation, smiles and handclasps of esteem. It should be shown to be a loving reality instead of a memory by patience, forbearance, courtesy, and kindness.

This theory of presumed confidence in the persistence of affection is one of the sad phases of married life. We should have roses of love, ever-blooming, ever-breathing perfume, instead of dried roses pressed in the family Bible, merely for reference, as a memorial of what was, instead of guarantee of what is. Matrimony too often shuts the door of life and leaves sentiment, consideration and chivalry on the outside. The feeling may possibly be still alive, but it does not reveal itself rightly; the rhymed poetry of loving has changed to blank verse and later into dull prose. As the boy said of his father: "He's a Christian, but he's not working much at it now." Love without manifestation does not feed the heart any more than a locked bread-box feeds the body; it does not illuminate and brighten the round of daily duties any more than an unlit lamp lightens a room. There is often such a craving in the heart of a husband or a wife for expression in words of human love and tenderness that they are welcomed no matter from what source they may come. If there were more courtships continued after marriage, the work of the divorce courts would be greatly lessened. This realization is often one of the things that come too late.

There are more people in this world hungering for kindness, sympathy, comradeship and love, than are hungering for bread. We often refrain from giving a hearty word of encouragement, praise or congratulation to some one, even where we recognize that our feelings are known, for fear of making him conceited or overconfident. Let us tear down these dykes of reserve, these walls of petty repression, and let in the flood of our feelings. There have been few monuments reared to the memory of those who have failed in life because of overpraise. There is more chiseled flattery on tombstones than was ever heard in life by the dead those stones now guard. Man does not ask for flattery, he does not long for fulsome praise, he wants the honest, ringing sound of recognition of what he has done, fair appreciation of what he is doing, and sympathy with what he is striving to do.

Why is it that death makes us suddenly conscious of a hundred virtues in a man who seemed commonplace and faulty in life? Then we speak as though an angel had been living in our town for years and we had suddenly discovered him. If he could only have heard these words while living, if he could have discounted the eulogies at, say even sixty per cent, they would have been an inspiration to him when weary, worn and worried by the problems of living. But now the ears are stilled to all earthly music, and even if they could hear our praise, the words would be but useless messengers of love that came too late.

It is right to speak well of the dead, to remember their strength and to forget their weakness, and to render to their memory the expressions of honor, justice, love and sorrow that fill our hearts. But it is the living, ever the living that need it most. The dead have passed beyond the helpfulness; our wildest cries of agony and regret bring no answering echo from the silences of the unknown. Those who are facing the battle of life, still seeking bravely to do and to be,—they need our help, our companionship, our love, all that is best in us. Better is the smallest flower placed in our warm, living hands than mountains of roses banked round our casket.

If we have failed in our expressions to the dead, the deep sense of our sorrow and the instinctive rush of feeling proclaim the vacuum of duty we now seek too late to fill. But there is one atonement that is not too late. It is in making all humanity legatees of the kindness and human love that we regret has been unexpended, it is in bringing brightness, courage and cheer into the lives of those around us. Thus our regret will be shown to be genuine, not a mere temporary gush of emotionalism.

It is during the formative period, the time when a man is seeking to get a foothold, that help counts for most, when even the slightest aid is great. A few books lent to Andrew Carnegie when he was beginning his career were to him an inspiration; he has nobly repaid the loan, made posterity his debtor a million-fold by his beneficence in sprinkling libraries over the whole country. Help the saplings, the young growing trees of vigor,—the mighty oaks have no need of your aid.

The heartening words should come when needed, not when they seem only hypocritic protestations, or dextrous preparations for future favors. Columbus, surrounded by his mutinous crew, threatening to kill him, alone amid the crowd, had no one to stand by him. But he neared land, and riches opened before them; then they fell at his feet, proclaimed him almost a god and said he truly was inspired from Heaven. Success transfigured him—a long line of pebbly beach and a few trees made him divine. A little patience along the way, a little closer companionship, a little brotherly love in his hours of watching, waiting, and hoping would have been great balm to his soul.

It is in childhood that pleasures count most, when the slightest investment of kindness brings largest returns. Let us give the children sunlight, love, companionship, sympathy with their little troubles and worries that seem to them so great, genuine interest in their growing hopes, their vague, unproportioned dreams and yearnings. Let us put ourselves into their places, view the world through their eyes so that we may gently correct the errors of their perspective by our greater wisdom. Such trifles will make them genuinely happy, happier by far than things a thousand times greater that come too late.

Procrastination is the father of a countless family of things that come too late. Procrastination means making an appointment with opportunity to "call again to-morrow." It kills self-control, saps mental energy, makes man a creature of circumstances instead of their creator. There is one brand of procrastination that is a virtue. It is never doing to-day a wrong that can be put off till to-morrow, never performing an act to-day that may make to-morrow ashamed.

There are little estrangements in life, little misunderstandings that are passed by in silence between friends, each too closely armored with pride, and enamoured with self to break. There is a time when a few straightforward words would set it all right, the clouds would break and the sunshine of love burst forth again. But each nurses a weak, petty sense of dignity, the rift grows wider, they drift apart, and each goes his lonely way, hungering for the other. They may waken to realization too late to piece the broken strands of affection into a new life.

The wisdom that comes too late in a thousand phases of life usually has an irritating, depressing effect on the individual. He should charge a large part of it to the account of experience. If no wisdom came too late there would be no experience. It means, after all, only that we are wiser to-day than we were yesterday, that we see all things in truer relation, that our pathway of life has been illuminated.

The world is prone to judge by results. It is glad to be a stockholder in our success and prosperity, but it too often avoids the assessments of sympathy and understanding. The man who pulls against the stream may have but a stanch two or three to help him. When the tide turns and his craft swiftens its course and he is carried along without effort, he finds boats hurrying to him from all directions as if he had suddenly woke up and found himself in a regatta. The help then comes too late; he does not need it. He himself must then guard against the temptation of cynicism and coldness and selfishness. Then he should realize and determine that what he terms "the way of the world" shall not be his "way." That he will not be too late with his stimulus to others who have struggled bravely as he has done, but who being less strong may drop the oars in despair for the lack of the stimulus of even a friendly word of heartening in a crisis.

The old song of dreary philosophy says: "The mill will never grind again with the water that is past." Why should the mill expect to use the same water over and over? That water may now be merrily turning mill-wheels further down the valley, continuing without ceasing, its good work. It is folly to think so much of the water that is past. Think more of the great stream that is ever flowing on. Use that as best you can, and when it has passed you will be glad that it came, and be satisfied with its service.

Time is a mighty stream that comes each day with unending flow. To think of this water of past time with such regret that it shuts our eyes to the mighty river of the present is sheer folly. Let us make the best we can of to-day in the best preparation for to-morrow; then even the things that come too late will be new revelations of wisdom to use in the present now before us, and in the future we are forming.

8. The Way of the Reformer

The reformers of the world are its men of mighty purpose. They are men with the courage of individual conviction, men who dare run counter to the criticism of inferiors, men who voluntarily bear crosses for what they accept as right, even without the guarantee of a crown. They are men who gladly go down into the depths of silence, darkness and oblivion, but only to emerge finally like divers, with pearls in their hands.

He who labors untiringly toward the attainment of some noble aim, with eyes fixed on the star of some mighty purpose, as the Magi followed the star in the East, is a reformer. He who is loyal to the inspiration of some great religious thought, and with strong hand leads weak trembling steps of faith into the glory of certainty, is a reformer. He who follows the thin thread of some revelation of Nature in any of the sciences, follows it in the spirit of truth through a maze of doubt, hope, experiment and questioning, till the tiny guiding thread grows stronger and firmer to his touch, leading him to some wondrous illumination of Nature's law, is a reformer.

He who goes up alone into the mountains of truth and, glowing with the radiance of some mighty revelation, returns to force the hurrying world to listen to his story is a reformer. Whoever seeks to work out for himself his destiny, the life-work that all his nature tells him should be his, bravely, calmly and with due consideration of the rights of others and his duties to them, is a reformer.

These men who renounce the commonplace and conventional for higher things are reformers because they are striving to bring about new conditions; they are consecrating their lives to ideals. They are the brave aggressive vanguard of progress. They are men who can stand a siege, who can take long forced marches without a murmur, who set their teeth and bow their heads as they fight their way through the smoke, who smile at the trials and privations that dare to daunt them. They care naught for the hardships and perils of the fight, for they are ever inspired by the flag of triumph that seems already waving on the citadel of their hopes.

If we are facing some great life ambition let us see if our heroic plans are good, high, noble and exalted enough for the price we must pay for their attainment. Let us seriously and honestly look into our needs, our abilities, our resources, our responsibilities, to assure ourselves that it is no mere passing whim that is leading us. Let us hear and consider all counsel, all light that may be thrown on every side, let us hear it as a judge on the bench listens to the evidence and then makes his own decision. The choice of a life-work is too sacred a responsibility to the individual to be lightly decided for him by others less thoroughly informed than himself. When we have weighed in the balance the mighty question and have made our decision, let us act, let us concentrate our lives upon that which we feel is supreme, and, never forsaking a real duty, never be diverted from the attainment of the highest things, no matter what honest price we may have to pay for their realization and conquest.

When Nature decides on any man as a reformer she whispers to him his great message, she places in his hand the staff of courage, she wraps around him the robes of patience and self-reliance and starts him on his way. Then, in order that he may have strength to live through it all, she mercifully calls him back for a moment and makes him—an optimist.

The way of the reformer is hard, very hard. The world knows little of it, for it is rare that the reformer reveals the scars of conflict, the pangs of hope deferred, the mighty waves of despair that wash over a great purpose. Sometimes men of sincere aim and unselfish high ambition, weary and worn with the struggle, have permitted the world to hear an uncontrolled sob of hopelessness or a word of momentary bitterness at the seeming emptiness of all effort. But men of great purpose and noble ideals must know that the path of the reformer is loneliness. They must live from within rather than in dependence on sources of help from without. Their mission, their exalted aim, their supreme object in living, which focuses all their energy, must be their source of strength and inspiration. The reformer must ever light the torch of his own inspiration. His own hand must ever guard the sacred flame as he moves steadily forward on his lonely way.

The reformer in morals, in education, in religion, in sociology, in invention, in philosophy, in any line of aspiration, is ever a pioneer. His privilege is to blaze the path for others, to mark at his peril a road that others may follow in safety. He must not expect that the way will be graded and asphalted for him. He must realize that he must face injustice, ingratitude, opposition, misunderstanding, the cruel criticism of contemporaries and often, hardest of all, the wondering reproach of those who love him best.

He must not expect the tortoise to sympathize with the flight of the eagle. A great purpose is ever an isolation. Should a soldier leading the forlorn hope complain that the army is not abreast of him? The glorious opportunity before him should so inspire him, so absorb him, that he will care naught for the army except to know that if he lead as he should, and do that which the crisis demands, the army must follow.

The reformer must realize without a trace of bitterness that the busy world cares little for his struggles, it cares only to joy in his final triumph; it will share his feasts but not his fasts. Christ was alone in Gethsemane, but—at the sermon in the wilderness, where food was provided, the attendance was four thousand.

The world is honest enough in its attitude. It takes time for the world to realize, to accept, and to assimilate a large truth. Since the dawn of history, the great conservative spirit of every age, that ballast that keeps the world in poise, makes the slow acceptance of great truths an essential for its safety. It wisely requires proof, clear, absolute, undeniable attestation, before it fully accepts. Sometimes the perfect enlightenment takes years, sometimes generations. It is but the safeguard of truth. Time is the supreme test, the final court of appeals that winnows out the chaff of false claims, pretended revelation, empty boast, and idle dreams. Time is the touchstone that finally reveals all true gold. The process is slow, necessarily so, and the fate of the world's geniuses and reformers in the balance of their contemporary criticism, should have a sweetness of consolation rather than the bitterness of cynicism. If the greatest leaders of the world have had to wait for recognition, should we, whose best work may be but trifling in comparison with theirs, expect instant sympathy, appreciation, and coöperation, where we are merely growing toward our own attainment?

The world ever says to its leaders, by its attitude if not in words, "If you would lead us to higher realms of thought, to purer ideals of life, and flash before us, like the handwriting on the wall, all the possible glories of development, you must pay the price for it, not we." The world has a law as clearly defined as the laws of Kepler: "Contemporary credit for reform works in any line will be in inverse proportion to the square root of their importance." Give us a new fad and we will prostrate ourselves in the dust; give us a new philosophy, a marvelous revelation, a higher conception of life and morality, and we may pass you by, but posterity will pay for it. Send your messages C.O.D. and posterity will settle for them. You ask for bread; posterity will give you a stone, called a monument.

There is nothing in this to discourage the highest efforts of genius. Genius is great because it is decades in advance of its generation. To appreciate genius requires comprehension and the same characteristics. The public can fully appreciate only what is a few steps in advance; it must grow to the appreciation of great thought. The genius or the reformer should accept this as a necessary condition. It is the price he must pay for being in advance of his generation, just as front seats in the orchestra cost more than those in the back row of the third gallery.

The world is impartial in its methods. It says ever, "you may suffer now, but we will give you later fame." Posthumous fame means that the individual may shiver with cold, but his grandchildren will get fur-lined ulsters; the individual plants acorns, his posterity sells the oaks. Posthumous fame or recognition is a check made out to the individual, but payable only to his heirs.

There is nothing the world cries out for so constantly as a new idea; there is nothing the world fears so much. The milestones of progress in the history of the ages tell the story. Galileo was cast into prison in his seventieth year and his works were prohibited. He had committed no crime, but he was in advance of his generation. Harvey's discovery of the circulation of the blood was not accepted by the universities of the world till twenty-five years after its publication. Frœbel, the gentle inspired lover of children, suffered the trials and struggles of the reformer, and his system of teaching was abolished in Prussia because it was "calculated to bring up our young people in atheism." So it was with thousands of others.

The world says with a large airy sweep of the hand, "the opposition to progress is all in the past, the great reformer or the great genius is recognized to-day." No, in the past they tried to kill a great truth by opposition; now we gently seek to smother it by making it a fad.

So it is written in the book of human nature: The saviours of the world must ever be martyrs. The death of Christ on the cross for the people he had come to save, typifies the temporary crucifixion of public opinion that comes to all who bring to the people the message of some great truth, some clearer revelation of the divine. Truth, right, and justice must triumph. Let us never close the books of a great work and say "it has failed."

No matter how slight seem results, how dark the outlook, the glorious consummation of the past, the revelation of the future, must come. And Christ lived thirty years and he had twelve disciples, one denied him, one doubted him, one betrayed him, and the other nine were very human. And in the supreme crisis of His life "they all forsook him and fled," but to-day—His followers are millions.

Sweet indeed is human sympathy, the warm hand-clasp of confidence and love brings a rich inflow of new strength to him who is struggling, and the knowledge that someone dear to us sees with love and comradeship our future through our eyes, is a wondrous draught of new life. If we have this, perhaps the loyalty of two or three, what the world says or thinks about us should count for little. But if this be denied us, then must we bravely walk our weary way alone, toward the sunrise that must come.

The little world around us that does not understand us, does not appreciate our ambition or sympathize with our efforts, that seem to it futile, is not intentionally cruel, calloused, bitter, blind, or heartless. It is merely that busied with its own pursuits, problems and pleasures, it does not fully realize, does not see as we do.

The world does not see our ideal as we see it, does not feel the glow of inspiration that makes our blood tingle, our eye brighten, and our soul seem flooded with a wondrous light. It sees naught but the rough block of marble before us and the great mass of chips and fragments of seemingly fruitless effort at our feet, but it does not see the angel of achievement slowly emerging from its stone prison, from nothingness into being, under the tireless strokes of our chisel. It hears no faint rustle of wings that seem already real to us nor the glory of the music of triumph already ringing in our ears.

There come dark, dreary days in all great work, when effort seems useless, when hope almost appears a delusion, and confidence the mirage of folly. Sometimes for days your sails flap idly against the mast, with not a breath of wind to move you on your way, and with a paralyzing sense of helplessness you just have to sit and wait and wait. Sometimes your craft of hope is carried back by a tide that seems to undo in moments your work of months. But it may not be really so, you maybe put into a new channel that brings you nearer your haven than you dared to hope. This is the hour that tests us, that determines whether we are masters or slaves of conditions. As in battle of Marengo, it is the fight that is made when all seems lost that really counts and wrests victory from the hand of seeming defeat.

If you are seeking to accomplish any great serious purpose that your mind and your heart tell you is right, you must have the spirit of the reformer. You must have the courage to face trial, sorrow and disappointment, to meet them squarely and to move forward unscathed and undaunted. In the sublimity of your perfect faith in the outcome, you can make them as powerless to harm you, as a dewdrop falling on the Pyramids.

Truth, with time as its ally, always wins in the end. The knowledge of the inappreciation, the coldness, and the indifference of the world, should never make you pessimistic. They should inspire you with that large, broad optimism that sees that all the opposition of the world can never keep back the triumph of truth, that your work is so great that the petty jealousies, misrepresentations, and hardships caused by those around you, dwindle into nothingness. What cares the messenger of the king for his trials and sufferings if he knows that he has delivered his message? Large movements, great plans, always take time for development. If you want great things, pay the price like a man.

Any one can plant radishes; it takes courage to plant acorns and to wait for the oaks. Learn to look not merely at the clouds, but through them to the sun shining behind them. When things look darkest, grasp your weapon firmer and fight harder. There is always more progress than you can perceive, and it is really only the outcome of the battle that counts.

And when it is all over and the victory is yours, and the smoke clears away and the smell of the powder is dissipated, and you bury the friendships that died because they could not stand the strain, and you nurse back the wounded and flint-hearted who loyally stood by you, even when doubting, then the hard years of fighting will seem but a dream. You will stand brave, heartened, strengthened by the struggle, re-created to a new, better and stronger life by a noble battle, nobly waged, in a noble cause. And the price will then seem to you—nothing.

Printed in Great Britain
by Amazon

40155297R00056